31 Days of

Prayer

for Your

Future Husband

Becoming a Wife Before the Wedding Day

Connect with us!

Website:

waitingforyourboaz.com

Facebook:

facebook.com/waitingforyourboaz

Twitter:

twitter.com/waiting_on_boaz

Pinterest:

pinterest.com/waitingonboaz

Contact Us:

waitingforyourboaz@hotmail.com

To my husband, Kevin-

I cannot thank God enough for bringing along my soul mate. I love you and cherish you deeply.

TABLE OF CONTENTS

PART ONE:

A CALL TO DIVINE LOVE

Trust the Author of Love with your Love Story..............................8

Becoming a Modern Day Ruth.............................16

The Power of a Praying Woman..........................21

PART TWO:

31 DAYS OF PRAYER FOR YOUR FUTURE HUSBAND

31 Days of Prayer...............31

About the Author..............124

PART ONE:

A CALL TO

DIVINE

LOVE

TRUST THE AUTHOR OF LOVE WITH YOUR LOVE STORY

Praying for the person you are going to marry is the most important thing you can do for them during your season of singleness.

Prayer is powerful and paves the way for both of you to come together in God's perfect

8

timing. Prayer produces growth and maturation in both your heart, and the heart of your future husband.

While some are called to a lifetime of marriage to the Lord, others are called to serve God with a helpmate. Your helpmate is the spouse God has set aside for you.

Have ever wrestled with the question; *Does God have someone for me?* If you have, I want you to take this tidbit of peace and place it down deep within your heart; If you have a desire for marriage, I truly believe that is something God has placed in you for a reason. I believe it is an utter beckoning from God, giving you clues to His will for your life and preparing your heart for what is to come.

I truly feel that if you weren't meant to marry, that desire wouldn't have been placed by God within you. The Apostle Paul spoke to the people in Corinth and told them that if you can remain single and serve that Lord, that is the simplest lifestyle. Yet he also states (as a concession and not as a commandment) that it is *"better to marry than to burn with passion."* (1 Corinthians 7:9) He also goes on to say that, *"each one has his own gift from God, in whatever manner that may be."*

When you fall in love with God and commit your ways to Him, He places His desires for your life in your heart.

Daily as you walk closer, you will notice that the yearnings of your heart begin to align with His. The closer you walk, the further in love you fall with the Savior and begin to understand His will for your life. Your heart begins to take on the character of the heart of Jesus.

If you were not meant to marry, you would feel fully content remaining single and devoting your entire life to loving and serving your first love, Jesus. And while your heart should be committed to that extent, there is nothing wrong with having a desire to marry the man God has for you, as the both of you devote your entire lifetime to chasing after and serving your First Love.

Unfortunately, many choose not to wait on the person God has for them. It is easy to make rash decisions out of desperation and loneliness. We live in a microwave society where we've been taught that we shouldn't have to wait for anything. We desire instant gratification. We want what we want, when we want it. To wait for anything, let alone love, makes us feel uncomfortable. We've been trained to think that being alone for any amount of time is unacceptable.

The reason so many people miss out on their blessing is because they decide to settle for a microwave dinner instead of waiting on the feast God has for them. The best things really do take time. It's important to remember that God is not only preparing your future husband, but He is preparing you as well. And when the time comes, God will bring you both together and it will be greater and more beautiful than you could have ever imagined.

God is the author of love. He is the embodiment of love. When we choose to hand over the pen and let God write our love story, we are choosing the divine will of God. When I gave my heart to God as a young girl, I didn't understand all that God had in store for my life. At a young age I discovered that He was the missing piece to my heart and He was what I needed to feel the contentment I had been searching for my whole life. I fell in love with Jesus, and our romance blossomed daily as He revealed His wondrous love for me.

As I grew closer to God, He began impressing on my heart that He had more for me than just my salvation. He wanted to take care of me and bless every single area of my life for the simple fact that He loved me and I am His cherished daughter.

He wanted to bless me with the kind of love story that only He could give, just like He wants to bless you with the desires of your heart. So I gave Him the pen, and let Him do His work within me and in my life.

I truly believe you can come to a place in God where you are fully satisfied in him. But I also believe it is a natural God-given desire to dream about finding your soul mate. I went back and forth between both of those places constantly. There were many times I felt fully content in my romance with Jesus, then I had my days, just like everyone else, where I longed for my helpmate, to love and serve God with.

If I had known then what I know now, I would've lifted up my concerns to God and left them there, trusting that He would perfect all that concerned me. I would've trusted without any doubt that He would bring along my Boaz on His timetable, not mine.

God deserves the number one spot in your heart. He wants to be your first love. He longs to love and woo you, and the love He gives outweighs that of a thousand lovers. If you don't listen to anything else I say, listen to this; fall in love with God first, and the rest will fall into place.

13

Seek after God relentlessly and passionately, and ask your Father to cause your desires to align with His will for your life. In doing so, He will reveal His will for your life. You may not understand the process, but your job is to trust the Author of the process.

God wants to bless you with a divine love, something that you couldn't go out and find on your own. So let the Author write your story and embrace each chapter and step along the way. Besides, your life doesn't begin when you find the right man, it begins the day you find Jesus.

The thing about waiting for your Boaz is that you aren't designed to just sit around and wait for someone feeling desperate and miserable. You are called to work, serve, and enjoy your life and relationship with Jesus, now and long after your Boaz comes into your life.

Precious daughter of God, please do not wish your invaluable life away. You were designed to fall in love with God, serve Him, love others, and live your life each day to the fullest. Everything that is ordained by God will come in His perfect timing and not a minute sooner.

BECOMING A MODERN DAY RUTH

A modern day Ruth refuses to conform to the patterns of this world. She refuses to let the world tell her that she's something she's not. She finds her identity in Christ.

She isn't like other women; she has been set apart, called out, chosen. She refuses to be a people pleaser; she is a God pleaser. She allows God to work through her and chooses to love and serve others while she waits.

She is so consumed in her love for God and the work she has been called to do that the wait doesn't feel like waiting. She isn't caught up in the process, but rather, she is patiently trusting God, the ruler of her heart, with all the days of her future.

She knows her season of singleness is for a reason and only a season. She doesn't know what the future holds, but she trusts the one who holds it. And when God brings her Boaz into her life, she still submits herself to the Lord follows His lead. She knows when to wait and when to move because she is in tune with the Holy Spirit's voice.

How does she discern what move to take? Every decision she makes is guided by prayer. Every move she makes is made in love and faithfulness. Her inner voice has become that of her Father's. She trusts Him with her entire life, no matter what the future may bring. Today you can make the decision to hand over the pen of your life and let God be the author of your love story.

We serve a God of new beginnings and second chances. His mercies are new every single morning. Your best days are yet to come. He has wonderful things in store for you and that doesn't just concern marriage. This promise concerns every single area of your life. Fall in love with God because He is passionately, remarkably, crazy in love with you.

He wants first place in our heart. Psalm 37:4 tells us, *"Delight in the Lord and He will give you the desires of your heart."* God has not called you to live a mediocre life. He doesn't want to just give you an "okay" job, or an "okay" marriage. He wants to bless you abundantly and cause your cup to overflow.

He wants to give you the best of everything, for the simple fact that He is your

Father and you are treasured. He is going to cause your cup to overflow with blessings and everyone around you is going to see the goodness of God in your life.

He wants to give you His perfect peace, but first you have to fix your eyes on Him. He is working everything out for your good. Hold onto your Father, cherished daughter. You are precious to Him and He delights in you. God is calling you into a passionate romance with Himself. He wants to give you a love story that will put all of the other fairytales you've read about to shame.

God has embedded those desires in your heart for a reason, and when the timing is right, He will bring those desires to fruition. You can trust that your heart is safe when you place it in the hands of God.

He will always take care of you. In this moment find tranquility in the fact that God has called you to be a modern day Ruth, to love and to serve until your Boaz comes into your life. Then when your Boaz comes, you will continue to love and serve God together for the rest of your days.

The Power of a Praying Woman

I am a firm believer that prayer can change the entire course of history. I have seen prayers move mountains. I've seen the sick healed, generational curses broken, and lives changed. Prayer is powerful. Prayer is our communication with God and it unleashes the floodgates of heaven.

Every decision you make should be made with godly discernment and prayer. There is no prayer too small for God. Is anything too hard for Him? He is concerned with every part of you.

He knows every single hair on your head. With that being said, it is okay to pour your desires and needs on God. In fact, He wants you to do that. He desires a committed relationship with you.

Christianity was never meant to be a set of rules. The true mark of a believer is an ongoing love affair with the one who created you. God cares about you and is madly in love with you. He cares about your well-being, and He cares about the person you are going to marry. He even cares about your future children and even your grandchildren. He is concerned with everything that concerns you.

The concept of praying for your future husband has been radicalized, but it is actually a very simple notion. We present every other matter in our life to God, so why shouldn't we pray for the person we will marry someday?

When we fall in love with God and realize how much He loves us, we then realize He cares about everything we are and will ever do, including our future spouse.

Not only that, but we are called to pray for our future spouse. I am a firm believer that my position as a wife and mother is my first calling. As a woman who deeply loves God, my husband, and daughter, I believe your family should be your priority, and your ministry starts at the homestead.

Your future husband needs your prayers. When you pray for your future husband, you are speaking life into your marriage even if you haven't even met him yet. You are speaking blessings and healing over him that will help to prepare Him to be the man that God has called him to be.

Prayer connects you to Him. Your prayers can save him from falling and encourage him when he desperately needs it. You may not know what he is going through at the moment, but your prayers could be what saves him. Praying for your future husband will also mold you into a powerful, Godly wife, even if there are no prospects in sight. The time to start preparing for your marriage is now.

Both you and your future husband are called to lift one another up in prayer and intercede on the other's behalf. Prayer connects you both in love. You are speaking your marriage into existence. Proverbs 18:21 tells us that, *"death and life lie in the power of the tongue."* That isn't something to take lightly.

Don't speak death over your life. Don't let the words utter from your mouth that you will never find the person God has for you or never get married. Rebuke any negativity that tries to enter your mind and soul and plead the blood of Jesus.

Speak life over everything and everyone in your path. Speak existence into your future marriage and family, and you can rest assured that God hears your prayers and is moving on behalf of the situation as He prepares both of your hearts for what's to come.

Marriage is a calling and blessing, so is your season of singleness. So many detest it, but it is a beautiful time of sole intimacy with Jesus as He prepares you to be the wife you are called to be.

1 Corinthians 2:9 tells us, *"Eye has not seen, nor ear heard, nor have entered into the heart of man The things which God has prepared for those who love Him."*

Praying for your future husband not only helps him to become the man of God and husband he is called to be, but it prepares you

to be the woman of God and wife that you are
called to be.

Learning to pray for your future husband
molds your character and teaches you to think
of others before yourself. It helps you to
comprehend that you are praying for a real
person, and causes you to have love for him in
your heart, even if you haven't met him yet.

Waiting for your future husband
becomes much easier when you realize this
isn't just some fairytale, it's a promise from
God. Respond to the call. Become a praying
wife, long before the wedding day. Pray for
your future husband every day.

Speak life over him. Rebuke chains that
would try to keep him bound. Pray for God to
reserve him. Prayer is the magnet that will
bring you both together and God is the glue
that will keep you both together.

These are prayers that I prayed over my
future husband, and I decided to share them

with you as a guideline to help you get started. However, keep in mind that praying for your future husband isn't something you should only do 31 days out of the year, it is something that you need to do every single day of the year.

If you aren't sure how to pray for him, I hope this book will serve as a guide on how to do so and spark a flame inside of your heart. When praying for your future husband and marriage, the most important thing is to speak from your heart and be led by the Holy Spirit on how to pray for him.

God will give you discernment on how to pray for him. When I was single I kept a journal to God, and I also kept one for my future husband for years. This helped me to get my thoughts and feelings down on paper and also kept me encouraged as I was waiting on God.

When I decided to trust God with my future marriage and do things His way, He taught me a lot about love. I came to the realization that my future husband didn't deserve the scraps left from my heart after I had given it away to every man that came before him. Instead, he deserved all of my love.

Your future husband deserves a wife who will love him, stand by him, and pray for Him. You deserve exactly the same. This devotional also gives you a chance to jot down your thoughts and prayers. Writing letters to your future husband will be a beautiful gift to the person you will marry someday and also help to keep you on the right path until you meet him.

I gave my journal to my husband on my wedding night. It was a beautiful gift of my devotion and faithfulness to both him and God through my season of singleness.

It now serves as a reminder to how faithful God truly is. This isn't just for women either, nothing gave me butterflies like receiving love letters from my husband, especially the ones he wrote to me before we even met each other.

The truest act of devotion to God is when you can lay down something in your life that you want to cling to so badly and trust that God will do what He said He will do. Waiting takes courage and patience. Waiting means putting your present desires aside for something greater down the road.

Waiting means forgetting the world's ideology of love and embracing the divine love that God has for you. Waiting means having a heart like Ruth, relentlessly pursuing God and living in full devotion to Jesus. The wait is always worth it. Trust and see what God has in store for you.

PART TWO:

31 DAYS

OF

PRAYER

Day One:

Prayer for His Spiritual Growth

"That you will walk in a manner worthy of the Lord, to please Him in all respects, bearing fruit in every good work and increasing in the knowledge of God;"

~Colossians 1:10

Heavenly Father,

As I begin this journey of praying for my future husband, I pray that you cultivate his heart, and that he would become all that you have called him to be. I pray that he would get on his knees and cry out to you, making an effort to seek you daily.

I pray that you would strengthen and mold him into a man of God who strives to live a life of purpose. I thank you for his spiritual growth. I thank you for helping him to become a mighty spiritual warrior and I pray that he would be faithful to you always.

In Jesus name,

Amen

MY PRAYER JOURNAL

_____

_____

_____

_____

Day Two:

Prayer for Provision

"Remember the Lord your God. He is the one who gives you power to be successful, in order to fulfill the covenant he confirmed to your ancestors with an oath."

~Deuteronomy 8:18

Heavenly Father,

Today I ask that you would give my future husband favor in every area of his life. Bless the work of his hands as he sows into his job, his future, and his ministry. I pray that every seed he has sown will bring forth a

34

bountiful harvest. I pray financial blessings upon him, that you would lead him with each step. I pray that He learns to rely on you in everything and to give according to how you have blessed him.

I pray that you would place in him a generous heart. Give him the resources he needs to carry out the task you have placed before him. Thank you for your provision and protection.

In Jesus name,

Amen

MY PRAYER JOURNAL

_____

_____

_____

DAY THREE:

PRAYER THAT HE WOULD GUARD HIS HEART

"Above all else, guard your heart, for everything you do flows from it."

~Proverbs 4:23

Heavenly Father,

Today I ask that you would guard my future husband's heart. Guard his mind from negativity, his eyes from perverseness, and his heart from anything that is not of you.

I pray that He would be rooted and established in love. When you bring us together, I pray that we would guard each other's hearts diligently and faithfully. I pray that He loves you faithfully and cries out to you in every circumstance and trial that he may face in this life.

In Jesus name,

Amen

My Prayer Journal

_____

_____

_____

_____

_____

DAY FOUR:

PRAYER FOR WISDOM

"For the Lord gives wisdom; from his mouth come knowledge and understanding."

~Proverbs 2:6

Heavenly Father,

Today I pray that you bless my husband with wisdom like Solomon. Give him eyes to see the things you would have him to see, and give him a heart to love the same way you love.

Let him speak boldly and with wisdom. Train him to be quick to listen, slow to speak,

40

and slow to become angry. I pray that he would come to you with every decision he has to make through careful consideration and your Holy Word.

In Jesus name,

Amen

MY PRAYER JOURNAL

_____

_____

_____

_____

_____

_____

DAY FIVE:

PRAYER FOR HIM TO BE STRENGTHENED

"But those who hope in the Lord will renew their strength. They will soar on wings like eagles; they will run and not grow weary, they will walk and not be faint."

~Isaiah 40:31

Heavenly Father,

Today I ask that you give my future husband strength in the face of adversity. Give him the strength to stand up for what is right

43

and to stand firm against the lies of the enemy.
I ask that you renew His strength and allow
Him to rest in your perfect peace. Love on him
today, and cause him to soar on wings like
eagles when his heart becomes overwhelmed.

In Jesus name,

Amen

MY PRAYER JOURNAL

_____

_____

_____

_____

_____

_____

45

DAY SIX:

PRAYER FOR HIS SAFETY

"The name of the Lord is a fortified tower; the righteous run to it and are safe."

~Proverbs 18:10

Heavenly Father,

Today I pray that you would place a hedge of protection around my future husband wherever he may go. I pray that wherever you would lead that he would follow.

I rebuke any curse or lifeless word that has been spoken over his life. I pray that he

46

would stay on the path you have called him
down and that he would remain safe in your
love for him. I thank you for provision and
protection on his life and heart.

In Jesus name,

Amen

MY PRAYER JOURNAL

_____

_____

_____

_____

_____

_____

DAY SEVEN:

PRAYER FOR HIS PREPARATION

"For I know the plans I have for you," declares the Lord. "Plans to prosper you and not to harm you, plan to give you a hope and a future."

~Jeremiah 29:11

Heavenly Father,

I pray today that you prepare my future husband's heart for all that is to come. Bless him with divine favor and reassure him that his future is bright.

Let each and every step he takes be taken in favor and grace. I pray that he has an impact on everyone he comes in contact with. Bless him generously and love on him today, Lord.

In Jesus name,

Amen

My Prayer Journal

_____

_____

_____

_____

_____

_____

DAY EIGHT:

PRAYER THAT HE WOULD WALK IN LOVE

"We have come to know and believed the love which God has for us. God is love, and the one who abides in love abides in God, and God abides in Him."

~1 John 4:16

Heavenly Father,

Today I pray that you would help my future husband to dwell and remain in love. I pray that his decisions would be guided by

52

your Holy Spirit and that he would be a walking, talking example of your precious love for us.

I pray he would love me and our future children just as you love the Church, as I strive to love him and become the wife he needs me to be. I thank you for your precious love.

In Jesus name,

Amen

MY PRAYER JOURNAL

_____

_____

_____

_____

DAY NINE:

PRAYER FOR HIS HEALTH

"He was pierced through for our transgressions, He was crushed for our iniquities; The chastening for our well-being fell upon Him, and by His scourging we are healed."

~Isaiah 53:5

Heavenly Father,

Today I pray for protection over my future husband's health. By your stripes we are healed, and I rebuke any sickness that would

try to enter his body or mind in your precious
name.

I pray that you would give him the
ability to make healthy decisions so that he
enjoy a life full of happiness and longevity. I
thank you for preserving his health.

In Jesus name,

Amen

MY PRAYER JOURNAL

_____

_____

_____

_____

_____

DAY TEN:

PRAYER THAT HE WOULD HAVE A FORGIVING HEART

"Get rid of all bitterness, rage and anger, brawling and slander, along with every form of malice. Be kind and compassionate to one another, forgiving each other, just as in Christ God forgave you."

~Ephesians 4:31-32

Heavenly Father,

Today I pray that my future husband would have the strength to let any and every

58

offense slide. I pray that instead of clinging to his pain, he clings to your love.

I pray he wouldn't let any seed of bitterness take root within his heart and that when he feels overwhelmed, he knows he will always have you by his side. Love him through the pain, and give him the strength to forgive.

In Jesus name,

Amen

MY PRAYER JOURNAL

_____

_____

_____

_____

DAY ELEVEN:

PRAYER FOR HIS INTEGRITY

---

*"A righteous man who walks in his integrity--
How blessed are his sons after him."*

~Proverbs 20:7

Heavenly Father,

Today I pray today that you would cause him to walk upright and to stand firm in his faith. Make his feet firm and continue strengthen his heart. I pray that he would choose integrity over popularity.

Teach him to walk in integrity and encourage his spirit. I thank you for the man of God you are molding him into.

In Jesus name,

Amen

My Prayer Journal

_____

_____

_____

_____

_____

_____

_____

63

Day Twelve:

Prayer for His Faith

"Delight yourself in the Lord and He will give you the desires of your heart."

~Psalm 37:4

Heavenly Father,

Today I ask that you bless my future husband with the ability to have faith in trying circumstances. I pray that he would take delight in you, and that you would give him the desires of his heart.

64

Protect him from anything sent to
destroy his faith. Grow him daily. Give him
the faith to trust in you, even when he can't see
what is in front of Him. Thank you for the
calling you've placed on his life and I pray that
in due time, you bring forth his destiny into
fruition.

In Jesus name,

Amen

MY PRAYER JOURNAL

_____

_____

_____

_____

_____

Day Thirteen:

Prayer for His Confidence

"For the LORD will be your confidence, and will keep your foot from being caught."

~Proverbs 3:26

Heavenly Father,

Today I pray that you would just love on my wonderful man of God today. Let him know he is loved and appreciated. Build his confidence and show him all that he is in you.

Let him know I love him already and am praying for him too. I pray that he would walk tall in confidence and in who you have called him to be. Teach him the ways of love, and guard his heart from insecurity and low self-esteem.

In Jesus name,

Amen

MY PRAYER JOURNAL

_____

_____

_____

_____

_____

_____

_____

DAY FOURTEEN:

PRAYER FOR FAVOR

---

*"May the favor of the Lord our God rest on us;
establish the work of our hands for us – yes,
establish the work of our hands."*

~Psalm 90:17

Heavenly Father,

Today I pray that you give my future husband unmerited favor in every area of his life. Lead him, guide him, and bless him in all he does. Do not let his foot slip, but establish the work of his hands.

70

Let him know it is not by his own power or ability, but that the glory always belongs to you. I pray that in every success he gives you all the glory and honor. I thank you Father for all that you are doing in his life.

In Jesus name,

Amen

MY PRAYER JOURNAL

_____

_____

_____

_____

_____

_____

Day Fifteen:

Prayer for Talent

"Each of you should use whatever gift you have received to serve others, as faithful stewards of God's grace in its various forms."

~1 Peter 4:10

Heavenly Father,

Today I ask you to bless my future husband's talents, that he would use them for your glory. Reveal new talents to him that he never knew he had. Multiply his talents.

Help him to grow daily to become better, stronger, and wiser. I pray he would always use the talents you have blessed him with to serve you and to help others. Lord, bless him and love on him today and always.

In Jesus name,

Amen

MY PRAYER JOURNAL

_____

_____

_____

_____

_____

_____

Day Sixteen:

Prayer Against Discouragement

"These things I have spoken to you, so that in Me you may have peace In the world you have tribulation, but take courage; I have overcome the world."

~John 16:33

Heavenly Father,

Today I rebuke discouragement from my future husband's heart and mind in Jesus name. Cause him to walk upright and to know who he is in you.

I pray you make all things work together for his good and that he would fall more in love with you every single day. I pray that he would take heed to the promptings of the Holy Spirit and that he always uses discernment in his decision making. Protect his heart, body, and spirit.

In Jesus name,

Amen

MY PRAYER JOURNAL

_____

_____

_____

_____

_____

DAY SEVENTEEN:

PRAYER FOR PARENTHOOD

"Behold, children are a gift of the LORD, the fruit of the womb is a reward. Like arrows in the hand of a warrior, so are the children of one's youth."

~Psalm 127:3-5

Heavenly Father,

Today I pray that if you see fit, that you would help my future husband to be a great father to our children someday. I pray that both of us together would set good examples for them.

I pray that through my future husband and I, our children will know what love looks like. I pray they see how in love we are with you, God. Help him to be the spiritual head and leader of our family.

In Jesus name,

Amen

MY PRAYER JOURNAL

_____

_____

_____

_____

_____

81

DAY EIGHTEEN:

PRAYER FOR HIS COMMUNICATION

"Do not let any unwholesome talk come out of your mouths, but only what is helpful for building others according to their needs, that it may benefit those who listen."

~Ephesians 4:19

Heavenly Father,

Today I ask that you help my future husband to control his tongue. I pray you show him what enormous damage it can do when he speaks out of anger.

I pray he uses his words to build and
encourage others, not to tear them down. I
pray he thinks before he speaks something,
and that he chooses to speak life and not death.
I thank you for preparing him to be a mighty
man of God.

In Jesus name,

Amen

MY PRAYER JOURNAL

_____

_____

_____

_____

_____

_____

Day Nineteen:

Pray for His Priorities

"But seek first his kingdom and his righteousness, and all these things will be given to you."

~Matthew 6:33

Heavenly Father,

Today I pray that you would help my future husband to manage his time. Help him, as the future head of our household, to keep his priorities straight even now, and to commit his time accordingly.

I pray that he would keep his focus on you, and seek your kingdom and righteousness as you provide everything he needs. Thank you for all of your blessings and for preparing my future husband for me.

In Jesus name,

Amen

My Prayer Journal

_____

_____

_____

_____

_____

_____

Day Twenty:

Prayer for Advisability

"Be angry and do not sin; do not let the sun go down on your anger, and give no opportunity to the devil."

~Ephesians 4:26

Heavenly Father,

Today I pray today that you help my future husband to maintain his self in stressful and compromising situations. I pray that he would make decisions guided by the Holy

88

Spirit so that every step he takes lines up with
your will for his life.

I pray that he would apply common
sense and rationality to his decisions, but
above all else, that he would follow your lead.
I thank you for calling and choosing my
husband.

In Jesus name,

Amen

My Prayer Journal

_____

_____

_____

_____

_____

Day Twenty-one:

Prayer for His Purity

"How can a young man keep his way pure? By guarding it according to your word."

~Psalm 119:9

Heavenly Father,

Today I pray that my future husband would cherish purity not only physically, but mentally as well. I pray that we would both only have eyes for each other.

I pray that you keep him on the narrow road and that daily he is learning to lean on you. Help us be devoted to one another and to you. Thank you for your faithfulness to us.

In Jesus name,

Amen

MY PRAYER JOURNAL

Day Twenty-two:

Prayer for His Relationships

"In your relationships with one another, have the same mindset as Christ Jesus."

~Philippians 2:5

Heavenly Father,

Today I pray that my future husband would have the same mindset as Christ Jesus when it comes to his relationships. I pray that you would set godly examples in his life to encourage and speak life into him.

I pray that you eliminate any toxic relationships that are holding him back from you. I pray you surround him with the right people who will encourage him to get to where he needs to be, and I pray he would do the same for them. Thank you Father for your blessings and calling on his life.

In Jesus name,

Amen

MY PRAYER JOURNAL

_____

_____

_____

_____

_____

Day Twenty-three:

Prayer to Stay on the Right Path

"I have directed you in the way of wisdom; I have led you in upright paths."

~Proverbs 4:11

Heavenly Father,

I pray that you would walk with my future husband daily. Keep him close to you. Fill him up with your unfailing love and peace. Teach him the paths of righteousness and lead him down the narrow road.

I pray that He stays on the right path, the one you have called him to walk. Let him know that you will love him through and through, no matter what life throws at him. You are great God, and I thank you in advance for blessing me with the man you have for me.

In Jesus name,

Amen

MY PRAYER JOURNAL

_____

_____

_____

_____

_____

Day Twenty-four:

Prayer for Obedience

"You shall walk after the Lord your God and fear Him, and keep His commandments and obey His voice, and you shall serve Him and cling to Him."

~Deuteronomy 13:4

Heavenly Father,

Today I pray that you surround my future husband with your love. I pray that he would be in tune with your heart and obedient to your voice.

100

I pray that he would dwell on your word and remain in prayer. I pray that he would cling to you and keep your commandments. I praise you for your unfailing love and divine favor on his life. Keep him close to you.

In Jesus name,

Amen

MY PRAYER JOURNAL

_____

_____

_____

_____

_____

_____

DAY TWENTY-FIVE:

PRAYER FOR HIS FRIENDSHIPS

"As iron sharpens iron, so one person sharpens another."

~Proverbs 27:17

Heavenly Father,

Today I pray that my future husband would choose his friends wisely. I pray that he would have a positive impact on everyone he comes in contact with.

I ask that you surround him with godly companions who will influence him to become a better man each day. As iron sharpens iron, so one man sharpens another. I thank you for strategically placing the right people along his path.

In Jesus name,

Amen

MY PRAYER JOURNAL

_____

_____

_____

_____

_____

_____

_____

DAY TWENTY-SIX:

PRAYER TO PURSUE CALLING

"Those He predestined, He also called; those He called, He also justified; and those He justified, He also glorified."

~Romans 8:30

Heavenly Father,

Today I ask that you would reveal my future husband's calling to him. Plant it deep in his heart. I pray that just like the prophet Jeremiah, his calling becomes a fire shut up in his bones.

106

Father, don't let him walk away from his calling. Instead, help him to grow and mature in it. Let him walk forth in his destiny just as you have designed him to do. Prepare him for what you have called him to do. I thank you for your unfailing love.

In Jesus name,

Amen

MY PRAYER JOURNAL

_____

_____

_____

_____

_____

_____

Day Twenty-seven:

Prayer for Vision

"Where there is no vision the people perish.
But happy is he who keeps the law."

~Proverbs 29:18

Heavenly Father,

Today I pray that you give my future husband eyes to see your divine will for his life. I pray that he would keep your laws, and that you would mature him into a man of God with heavenly vision.

109

I know your plans for him are great, and I pray you bring them into existence. I thank you for calling him, choosing him, and setting him apart.

In Jesus name,

Amen

MY PRAYER JOURNAL

_____

_____

_____

_____

_____

_____

Day Twenty-eight:

Prayer for Peace

"You will keep in perfect peace those whose minds are steadfast, because they trust in you."

~Isaiah 26:3

Heavenly Father,

Today I ask that you would cause my future husband's mind to be steadfast upon you. I pray that he has the ability to just rest in you, knowing that all things work together for the good of those who love the Lord.

Bless him with perfect peace that only you can give. I thank you for your joy, peace, grace, and mercy each day. Thank you for causing my future husband to abide in peace.

In Jesus name,

Amen

MY PRAYER JOURNAL

_____

_____

_____

_____

_____

_____

Day Twenty-nine:

Prayer for Financial Guidance

"And my God will meet all your needs according to the riches of his glory in Christ Jesus."

~Philippians 4:19

Heavenly Father,

Today I pray that you would give my future husband wisdom concerning his finances. I pray he would make smart financial choices in preparation for the future and that he would make sound, wise decisions

concerning our finances when you bring us
both together.

I pray that you would meet all of his
needs according to the riches of your glory.
Let your favor flow into every area of his life.

In Jesus name,

Amen

My Prayer Journal

_____

_____

_____

_____

_____

Day Thirty:

Prayer to Set Him Apart

---

*"You can be sure of this: The Lord set apart
the godly for himself. The Lord will answer
when I call to him."*

~Psalm 4:3

Heavenly Father,

Today I pray that you will give my future
husband the strength to not be influenced by
what others say, think, or feel about him. Give
him the grace to know that in you he is more
than a conqueror.

118

Help my future husband to live a victorious life in Christ Jesus and bless him this day, Lord. Empower him to speak your word and not to fear man. Set him apart and love on him today.

In Jesus Name,

Amen

My Prayer Journal

_____

_____

_____

_____

_____

_____

Day Thirty-one:

Prayer to Reserve His Heart

"Then the LORD God made a woman from the rib he had taken out of the man, and he brought her to the man."

~Genesis 2:22~

Heavenly Father,

I love you so much Papa. I thank you for the life of my future husband, and I will patiently wait until your perfect timing for us to come together. I will serve you while I wait, and I have faith now that it's already done because I have prayed with all my heart and I believe.

Reserve his heart for mine, and keep us both set aside for each other. Give him the courage and patience to choose your way over the world's way, and help us both to become the spouse we need to be for each other. We love you Father.

In Jesus name,

Amen

MY PRAYER JOURNAL

_____

_____

_____

_____

Tiffany Langford was born and raised in Somerset, Kentucky, but currently resides in Myrtle Beach, South Carolina with her husband and daughter. She is the founder of Waiting for your Boaz, a ministry dedicated to encouraging and loving women all over the globe. She blogs and ministers regularly. This is her first devotional.

Visit her blog at:
www.waitingforyourboaz.com

Made in the USA
Columbia, SC
01 October 2017